CONTENTS

Longman English Guides

HELP YOURSELF TO STUDY

Lesley Millard
Ralph Tabberer

Longman

Titles in the series

ABC of Common Errors *S H Burton*

Writing Letters *S H Burton*

Punctuation *Ian Gordon*

Spelling *S H Burton*

Help Yourself to Study *Lesley Millard Ralph Tabberer*

LONGMAN GROUP LIMITED
Longman House
Burnt Mill, Harlow, Essex, CM20 2JE, England
and Associated Companies throughout the world

First published 1985
ISBN 0 582 25073 0

Set in 10/11pt Linotron Rockwell Light and Medium

Produced by Longman Group (F.E.) Limited.
Printed in Hong Kong.

INTRODUCTION

Studying — it's a scream!

Most of us feel like this at some time. This book has ideas for helping you when you are studying. You may feel you are quite good at studying already, or you may feel that you are not. Whichever way it is, this book will help you to find and build on your strengths. As you work through the book, you will see that many of the things that you do every day (like finding the time of a favourite television programme in the newspaper) have given you skills you may not have realised you possess!

In this book, we remind you of the skills you have and show you more ways of using them.

Then you will be better equipped to **Help Yourself to Study.**

Suggestions about how to use this book

1 Skip through it all fairly quickly so that you get an idea of what it covers.
2 Try some of the exercises that appeal to you. Exercise sections have a line round them and are marked by this symbol:

Exercise

3 Decide what section you need at the moment or where you would find it easiest to start. (The questionnaire on pages 7–9 may help you decide where to begin or you may have a piece of work to do that you would like help with, eg an essay or some information you need to find.)

Even if you feel you need help with all or most of what the book covers, don't feel you need to work at more than one section at one time.

Refer back to the book when you have a study task to do — it can help at times when you feel a bit lost. Dip into the parts you need and leave the rest.

We hope you enjoy the book and find that studying can be fun!

QUESTIONNAIRE

Me as a learner

Read the questions and put a tick next to the answer you would give.

1 **What would you do if you were asked to work on a project which required collecting a lot of information? Would you:**

i try and forget about the whole thing until near the time it had to be finished?	ii go to the library in the hope that you will find something relevant?	iii try to sort out what you need to know and who to ask or where to look?
☐	☐	☐

2 **When you ask people questions, do you find that:**

i they usually understand immediately what you mean?	ii they miss the point so that you have to explain again?	iii after a short explanation they see what you mean?
☐	☐	☐

3 **When you have to do some reading, eg for homework, do you:**

i feel that you often waste some time on reading irrelevant sections?

ii look forward to doing some work on your own?

iii feel that as soon as you've read the book or article you've forgotten it all?

☐ ☐ ☐

4 **Imagine you're making notes from a book or lecture you attend, or from a video recording. Do you:**

i frequently feel fed up?

ii enjoy it once you get going?

iii get on with it because it has to be done?

☐ ☐ ☐

5 **You have to write an essay to hand in at 9.00 am tomorrow. Do you:**

i think of a good excuse for not doing it?

ii start to write even though you are not really clear about what you want to say?

iii spend time thinking about how you're going to tackle it and what you want to write?

☐ ☐ ☐

6 When you've done a piece of work and had it marked, do you:

i often feel that the mark is fair and what you expected?

ii sometimes feel surprised and upset at the mark you have?

iii feel that you have no idea why you got the mark you received?

☐   ☐   ☐

7 When you are studying do you:

i frequently feel fed up?

ii enjoy it once you get going?

iii get on with it because it has to be done?

☐   ☐   ☐

8 When it comes to exams do you:

i feel panicky, not manage to revise enough and do badly?

ii get a bit worried but get down to revising in time?

iii do some revision but never as much as you'd hoped to and not do as well as you feel you could have done?

☐   ☐   ☐

How did you get on?

Put a circle round the letter in the answer column (i, ii, or iii) you have chosen in each case.

Question	Answer i	Answer ii	Answer iii
1	A	B	C
2	C	A	B
3	B	C	A
4	A	C	B
5	A	B	C
6	C	B	A
7	A	C	B
8	A	C	B

If you scored a lot of As you may feel that studying is not enjoyable and you may not realise how many skills you already have. We hope that you will find nearly all the sections of the book useful. Start with the part of the book which looks most interesting, judging from your first quick flip through.

If you scored a lot of Bs you are getting to grips with studying but need help with building up your skills. We hope that the book will help you to do this.

If you scored a lot of Cs many of your skills are well developed but there may be a few areas where you feel you need some help. Dip into the sections of the booklet which you feel will help you.

If you scored a mixture of As, Bs and Cs look through your answers, see where you scored an A — that could show you where to start in the booklet. You already have some well-developed study skills but there are also areas where you feel some guidance could help you.

INFORMATION

When people ask you to 'look something up' or 'find out about something or someone', they are asking you to find **information.** When you look in a newspaper to find out what's on television, or ask a Job Centre about getting work you are asking for **information.**

Information tells you things

You will usually find it in the form of **words** (both spoken and written), **pictures** (photographs, slides, video and television), **numbers** (telephone numbers, figures), or **symbols.**

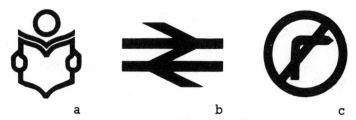

a	b	c

Do these symbols give you **information?** They should do, especially if you have met them before.* **Information** in all these forms helps us to *answer questions, make decisions* and *solve problems.* It is essential to studying. In fact, a great deal of studying is simply about making **information** your own.

---

* **a** is the symbol of the Literacy Scheme.
  b is for British Rail.
  c is the traffic instruction 'No right turn'.

Asking questions

Each of us uses questions as a way of getting information; for example:

HOW
- do I find out how to fix my bike?
- can I get a ticket for the match?

WHERE
- can I learn about photography?
- is the bus station?

WHEN
- are people old enough to buy things on hire purchase?
- did the Space Shuttle make its first flight?

WHICH
- is the easiest route between A and B?
- famous scientist won the Nobel Prize for Physics in 1921?

WHAT
- benefits am I entitled to if I can't find a job?
- is a microcomputer?

WHO
- can advise me about my legal rights?
- invented the long-playing record?

WHY
- don't I do very well in exams?
- do fish have gills?

The questions you ask are very important because they have a big effect on the **information** you receive. If you can ask *good questions* you will find it easy to handle **information**.

Good questions are carefully worded so that you get the answer you need.

Look back through those questions on page 12. All the words in capitals are words we use when asking for **information**. It can help to remember HOW, WHERE, WHEN, WHICH, WHAT, WHO and WHY. (**Note** there are six words starting with W, so HOW is the odd one out.) If you can think up and write different questions on a topic, you will be more able to pick out what a good question would be for you.

Exercise

Choose the questions which *you* think would get the information required. Underline the questions you choose.

Information required	Questions
1 To see if it will be OK to borrow the car between 7 and 10.30 pm on Tuesday	a 'Are you using the car on Tuesday evening?'
	b 'Is it all right if I borrow the car on Tuesday for the evening?'
2 The name of the first woman in space	a 'What's the name of that woman astronaut?'
	b 'What was the first woman in space called?'
	c 'Who was the first female cosmonaut?'
3 The chemical formula for sulphuric acid	a 'How do you write sulphuric acid using chemical symbols?'
	b 'How do you write sulphuric acid in chemistry?'
4 To be able to record a programme on a video recorder	a 'Have we got an instruction book for the video?'
	b 'Do you know how to use the video recorder?'
	c 'Will you show me how to set the video recorder before I go out at 6.30?'

Can you produce questions that are better than these?

13

Be clear

Notice what questions people ask you. How often do they ask the question that they really want answered? How often do they expect you to guess what they are really after? You may find a friend rings and says, 'Are you busy tonight?' but means to ask you to spend the evening with a group of friends. The actual question may not ever get asked!

Be precise

Think about what you really want to know before you ask a question. It also helps others to understand if you ask your question clearly. For example, don't say 'what?' if you mean 'who?' Be as precise as you can. This is as true when you're studying as it is anywhere else.

And, remember, you already have the answers to many questions. It's surprising how much information each of us has stored in our head. Complete the following sentences.

1 I know how ....
2 I know when ....
3 I know what ....
4 I know who ....
5 I know where ....
6 I know why ....
7 I know which ....

Exercise

Write down three questions to which you would really like the answer.

Re-write them if necessary until you are satisfied that you have made each question as clear as you can.

Think about what made this task easy or difficult for you.

If it was difficult you can practise again or find someone to practise swapping questions with. Make sure you answer precisely what you are asked!

Finding information

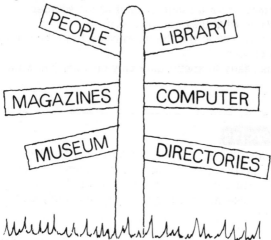

Information is here, there and everywhere. Of all the **information sources,** four types are most common:
PEOPLE
PUBLICATIONS
ORGANISATIONS
ELECTRONIC SOURCES

PEOPLE may include friends, experts, teachers and doctors.

PUBLICATIONS will include books and magazines, or microfiche, tape recordings, film, and photographs.

ORGANISATIONS may include libraries, Citizens' Advice Bureaux, and local government departments.

ELECTRONIC SOURCES will include television programmes, or Prestel, Ceefax and Oracle.

15

To find and use information well, it helps:
- to know about a range of information sources
- to know what they can give you
- to know how to get the information from the sources you choose
- to be ready to spend time only on what you want

Exercise

Jot down what sources of information *you* have used over the past month. (Don't forget yourself.) Underline those you use often. Put a circle around any that you'd like to use more but don't feel completely confident about.

We all use many sources of information — in order to get to work or school, to find out what's on television, to check how to use a hair dye, to discover the price of a packet of biscuits, and a whole host of other things.

Getting information from people

People are often the most convenient information sources. We use them every day. They often provide a very quick response to a question or problem, eg:

'What's the time?'
'How can I find the bus station?'
'How many points do I need to win?'
'What can I do about this greasy mark on my coat?'
'Can I get my money back on this record?'

You need to find the right person to ask, of course. This means judging who is likely to have the information you want.

The big advantage of using people as information sources is that you can have a two-way conversation with them. This helps you to get the right question and to decide what you really want. Here's an example of how this two-way process can work:

'What's on the TV tonight?'
'Nothing much.'
'I don't want your opinion, I want to know what's on.'
'Well, what are you interested in?'
'Is there a film?'
'Which channel?'
'Any one. I don't mind.'
'Well, there's a documentary filmed in Nicaragua on BBC 1 at 9.25, or there's a science fiction film on 2 at 10 past 10, or ITV's got a western based on a true story . . .'

The example shows how important it is to ask the right question. How you ask can also be very important. Usually, a friendly and polite approach encourages a friendly and helpful answer. The approach may make the information-giver more prepared to spend time ensuring that (a) he or she is clear about what you are asking, and (b) you understand the reply.

Getting information from publications

Books, magazines, tapes, slides and films are some of the published materials from which we can get information.

When you search for information from published materials, be aware of key words in order to get what you want. If you are looking for information about the ways snakes move and eat, you will probably find yourself flicking through published materials keeping your eye open for the key word, *snakes*. When you find something on snakes you probably start to use the next key words: *move* and *eat*.

Be aware of KEY WORDS. They can help you by being in the title of something published. They can help by being

17

in an index (see page 61) or on a contents page. Be prepared to alter your KEY WORDS if at first they don't seem to help. If you can't find something on snakes, it may help to change your KEY WORD to something similar (eg *serpent*), something which describes them (eg *reptile*), or even something which is an example of them (eg *adder*). Or think of alternative words which books may use; for example, if you look up *move* and *eat* you may find little, but if you look up *movement*, *motion*, *consumption*, *ingestion* or *food* you may find more.

Some people use **star patterns** to help them create their own KEY WORDS and ideas. For example, imagine you are doing a project on *housing* and you want to find examples of different sorts of housing in your home town. You may start with *housing* as your key word but not find enough.

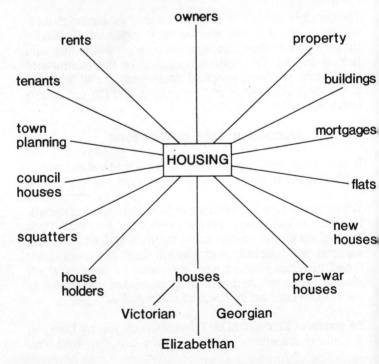

The next step could then be to shift to new key words. Perhaps if you write down in a star pattern all the possible key words you can think of, you may be well prepared to move on. We tried a pattern on housing for ourselves:

A star pattern may (a) be a way of thinking round a topic and giving you ideas, and (b) give you enough key words to find what you need.

Exercise

Have a go at a star pattern for the word *birthday*. Don't spend too much time at the start on any one word. Just jot down what comes to mind and then see what you've got. We have put in some rays to start but add as many as you want.

If you've enjoyed this, try the exercise again with a topic of your own choice, or one that you have to write about for an essay or project. It can be surprising how much you can jot down even on topics which you think you know nothing about!

Keep clearly in mind what you are looking for when using any publication.

REMEMBER that not all that is published is true!
It may be important to:
(a) **check the date of publication,** before you spend time on it (the date is usually given very near the start or the end, or on the packaging) — remember that some information, eg that on space technology, can quickly go out-of-date;

(b) **check the source.** Is it a fact or one person's opinion? Is it produced by someone who has a special view they wish to put over? Have things been left out in order to mislead you?

Published information, just like PEOPLE, ORGANISATIONS and ELECTRONIC SOURCES can be wrong!

Getting information from organisations

Some of the people who give us information provide it on behalf of an organisation. Organisations often organise carefully the information they have. You may need to discover how they organise it.

Libraries, museums, private firms, careers services, Job Centres, and the **Post Office** are good examples of organisations providing a mass of information.

Libraries are careful about organising what they have. They put their vast stores of information into systems which can help their users get what they want quite quickly and easily. The system many libraries use is known as the Dewey Decimal System.

Dewey Decimal System

It is a system you will probably know already. Materials in the library — those that aren't fiction — are given numbers up to (but not including) 1000. The numbers give you an indication of the sort of information the materials contain. Suppose a book has 598.2 on it. Because the number is between 500 and 600, the information is connected with *science*. Because the number is between 588 and 599, it is about *zoology*. If you look up books with this number you will find they are in fact on *birds*. The system helps you find information efficiently.

The librarian

You can always fall back on a person as a source of information and help in the library. The librarian will often help you find your way around the system or even get you exactly what you ask for. If you use people as information sources especially well, you may find that you rarely have to use the system itself. If not, then like most of us you'll gradually have to get used to the layout of libraries and the ways their contents are set out.

Exercise

If you are not very familiar with your libraries, visit your nearest library and find the 'Subject Catalogue'. It may be in booklet form, it may come as a computer printout, or on a number of cards in drawers or boxes. Look up the word *'study'*. Write down the classification number (in full). Try to find a book on the shelf which has the number. If you get stuck, ask a librarian to help.

If you want to repeat the exercise, choose a subject of interest or importance to you. Repeat the exercise above until you know your way around a bit more. Browse too, so that you can get some idea of what this information store contains.

If you enjoy browsing, you may find museums an attractive information source.

Museums will have a considerable amount of material on direct display (more will be stored elsewhere, and you'll have to ask to find out what and where) in the form of bones, pottery, garments, weapons, photographs, etc. Labels, short descriptions, catalogues will perhaps give you more information about the displays. As in a library, it helps to find out how material has been arranged and organised (they may say 'classified').

21

Private firms and **government departments** also give out
information. You may need to visit them and use the people
in them as direct sources of information. Sometimes, it may
be necessary to write. If you write, remember to ask clear,
precise questions.

A   14 Mayfield Road,
                         Nottingham.

                         27 February 1985

Dear Sir,

I am currently doing a project on smoking and the effects of advertising. I would like to know if you have any figures which show a relationship between the amount your firm spends on advertising and the sale of your cigarettes.

This project is part of my modern studies work at Berryfield Comprehensive School and I need to finish it by the end of May. I hope you will be able to reply fairly soon.

Yours faithfully,

Jane Kahn

B   9 Mayfield Road,
                         Nottingham.

                         27 February 1985

Dear Sir/Madam,

I am investigating links between the money spent on advertising by cigarette manufacturers and their sales figures.

Can you please send me any information you have on this? I would be very grateful for any help you can give me.

Yours faithfully,

Brenda Braithwaite

Reply 1　　　　　　　　　　　T.O.B. Tobacco plc,
　　　　　　　　　　　　　　　　Nottingham.

　　　　　　　　　　　　　　　　20 March 1985

Dear ＿＿＿＿＿＿＿＿＿,

Thank you for your letter. I am pleased to send you a copy of the report produced in 1982 by the Consumer Council, which discusses the role of advertising in the cigarette manufacturing industry.

I trust this will meet your requirements.

Yours sincerely,

John Philip

Reply 2　　　　　　　　　　　T.O.B. Tobacco plc,
　　　　　　　　　　　　　　　　Nottingham.

　　　　　　　　　　　　　　　　20 March 1985

Dear ＿＿＿＿＿＿＿＿＿,

Thank you for your letter. We are always pleased to help people in our local community.I am sending you an extract from a recent internal report which provides details of our expenditure on advertising over the past five years. I also enclose extracts from our last report to our shareholders which gives our sales figures over the same period.

Good luck with your project.

Yours sincerely,

John Philip

When you have made your choice, jot down two reasons for it. Take a close look at your reasons because they will probably give you important clues about how to get information from organisations.

Getting information from electronic sources

Television brings us a wealth of information and, in recent years, the VIEWDATA and TELETEXT services have become widely available. VIEWDATA and TELETEXT provides the public with information and at present comes in three main forms: CEEFAX, ORACLE and PRESTEL.

CEEFAX and ORACLE provide hundreds of pages of writing (or 'text') on the screen, and in many ways are like newspapers on the television. PRESTEL is a much larger computer service, containing a huge library of material for your television screen (provided you have the right telephone link), and it is able to 'converse' with you. You can use it to obtain news, get business information, order things you want, ask questions and receive replies.

The same things that help us to get information from other sources work with a whole range of electronic sources, including the most sophisticated computers:

- make sure you ask good questions
- use whatever clues you can
- try to become familiar with the different sources and the ways they work

Ask good questions

It is usually harder to browse through information stored electronically because of the time involved. It would take a lot of time for some information stores (or 'databases') to be flashed up piece by piece on a screen.

You will want to find something in particular and so, asking good questions matters. Often the electronic source will help you by offering you questions, or answers:

'What?'

'Key 1 to continue.'

'Do you want to try again?'

'What is your personal number?'

But you still have to make decisions.

There are times when the questions are irritating. This is when you must think hard about what you want and what the source can give you. You may be irritated because the database does not possess your answer. The information may not exist or the source may not be organised well enough to help you. So, with electronic sources as with others, think about your questions and keep an eye on what the system is likely to contain, or *not* contain. This brings us on to 'clues'.

Use the clues

Electronic sources are organised. There will be a system to them, and that system gives you clues to its use. Databases, or information stores, will have titles just like books. If a title doesn't sound right, look somewhere else. Databases will occasionally be described briefly, perhaps on paper that comes with the software you have.

The contents page and an index can help you get around in a book. Similarly, many electronic sources will be hard to use without the help of the contents list or index in some form. You can use the contents and index for more than just finding things — you can also use them to give you clues as to how useful the overall source is likely to be. With a book, you are sometimes wise to keep in mind when it was published (it will normally tell you near the front of the book, on the back of a title page). Similarly if you use a database, say with economic statistics or business figures, it may help to know whether or not it is up-to-date.

Practice helps you to become familiar with information sources. It's worth spending time in getting used to unfamiliar sources like PRESTEL, CEEFAX and ORACLE.

HELP YOURSELF TO READ BETTER

What do you read and how do you read it?

In order to study well you need to read flexibly. This means using different reading techniques for different purposes. Most readers use a variety of reading skills in their every-day lives, but it is sometimes difficult to see how these skills can be used for formal study. Start by thinking about the huge range of things you may already read.

Consider those that *you* read. Do you read them all

- in the same way?
- at the same speed?
- carefully and in detail?
- starting at the beginning and going on to the end?

Thinking about these questions will probably convince you that you do read different things in different ways. This means that you already read flexibly.

Problems with reading for study

You may feel you don't read flexibly when you study. You may not be using all the skills you have. The reasons for this can be:

1 Lack of familiarity

The books or other materials you read when you are studying are often less familiar than magazines, books or other things you read in everyday life. We all feel more confident about using things with which we are familiar.

2 Forgetting exactly why you are reading something

In everyday life, you tend to read things because you are interested, or you need to find something out in order to know where to go (reading a map) or what to do (reading instructions for setting up a video recorder). It is usually easy to decide what to concentrate on and what to leave out. It may be harder when you are studying, especially if you are doing a task you have been told to do and using books or other materials that someone else has suggested. It may be difficult to keep in mind exactly what your purpose is in doing a piece of reading and if you lose sight of your purpose you may well waste time and effort.

LACK OF FAMILIARITY WITH THE MATERIAL AND LOSING SIGHT OF YOUR PURPOSE MAY PREVENT YOU FROM USING YOUR FLEXIBLE READING SKILLS.

This exercise will help to show you what we mean about flexibility and purpose.

Exercise

Choose a story (from either a book or a magazine) that you have read and enjoyed. Choose one person in the story and flick through it to find three things which you can say about that person. Limit yourself to five minutes to get this done.

When you have finished, think about how you worked.

1 You will not have gone through the story in the same way as you did when you first read it. This should remind you that you can read in different ways. This doesn't mean that this quick way is a good way to read a story but it does show what is possible!

---

2 You will probably have found three things to say about the character you chose. You may not be happy about what you can say, and you may worry that you have not been accurate or that you could have said better things. Remember that the important thing in this exercise was finding three things you could say in a very short time. If you've done that, you have succeeded and proved to yourself that you can discover things without necessarily reading everything or reading slowly and carefully. You've also shown yourself that being very clear about what you want to know — your purpose — saves time and trouble.

Overcoming the problems

REMEMBER that when you are reading:
- **YOU HAVE THE CHOICE OF HOW YOU READ** (eg whether you skip over parts, whether you go slowly).
- **YOU DECIDE WHAT YOU ARE READING FOR** (eg to get an overview, to find a particular fact, to study one character in depth).

Decide why you are reading and how you are going to read before you start.

Ways of becoming more familiar with what you have to read

This section suggests ways in which you can become quite quickly at home with unfamiliar reading material and makes two key points:

1 Similar things to read tend to have similar layouts.

2 The material will contain clues to help you get an idea of what it's about.

Layout — the way something is organised
Take NEWSPAPERS as an example:
If you see one particular newspaper regularly you will find
that there tends to be a certain order to the contents. This
order doesn't change a great deal from day to day and
week to week.

Exercise

Think of a newspaper you see regularly. Without looking at the paper, jot down the answers to these questions (write a page number or a few words to show
what part of the paper you mean, eg 'very near the
middle', or 'the back page or next to the back page').

1 Where is the sports section?
2 Where are the cartoons?
3 Where is the TV/Radio information?
4 Where is the information about the weather?
5 What are your favourite parts of the paper?

Check your answer by looking at a copy of the paper.

If you looked at another newspaper now, you would find
that your answers would be slightly different, but probably
not very different. This shows that similar materials (newspapers) have a similar layout.

It's useful to bear this in mind when your study involves
reading, and to see if the things you already know will help
you find your way around new material. For example, if you
have found when using one book that it had very useful summaries at the end of each chapter, it's worthwhile checking
a new book to see whether it also has these summaries.
Similarly, once you've practised using the index which
comes at the back of many text books, you will find you can
often save time by turning straight to it when you need to
find a particular piece of information.

This is a short exercise to help explain this point:

Exercise

Find a book with an index. Choose from the index one word which can be found somewhere in the third or fourth chapter of the book. Give a friend or relative the book and ask them to find on what page the word you have chosen occurs. Watch what they do and compare their way of finding the word with your way.

Clues to what papers, magazines, books and articles contain

Take MAGAZINES as an example:

In magazines there are clues which help you to find what you are looking for without reading the whole thing.

Exercise

Find a magazine and look for the list of contents. See if this is very brief, eg

     Holidays . . . . . pages 7–9

or whether it gives you more information, eg

     Holidays — a look at family holidays in Europe on a tight budget . . . . . . pages 7–9.

Compare the contents page in your magazine to the contents page of a non-fiction book. Which has the more useful one? Decide which contents page you find (a) more informative and (b) easier to use. Jot down a few reasons for your decision.

(**Note:** the more informative may not be the easier one to use!)

Magazines use headings to attract your attention and help you to decide whether you want to read a particular section. Some books use headings too. Look at the headings in this book and decide what makes them useful.

The clues that appear in magazines, also appear in possibly less familiar materials such as text books. We've already mentioned contents pages and we said that part of the layout of most text books is an index at the back. The contents page and the index provide clues about the content of the book.

You can use these hints to decide whether you want to spend time on the book or not. For instance, the contents page may not mention the topic on which you need information, or anything related to that topic. If this is the case, you can probably safely decide you need not spend any time reading the book.

Try these exercises to help you to think about clues to what is in something you have to read.

Exercise

We've made a list of some of the things which provide clues about the materials you use. Read it through. Jot down any other sources of clues you can think of, then turn the page over and see how many things on the list you can remember.

contents page
headings
index
'blurb' on back cover
'blurb' on paper cover, inside the front of a book
summaries before or after chapters
information about the author
date of publication

Reasons for reading

If you spend a little time deciding exactly what you want to get from your reading before you start, you will save time and effort later on.

Why do people read things?

These are perfectly good reasons, but they are not very detailed. They do not give much information about what each person wants to get out of doing the reading. If you can have a clear sense of what you want to get from your reading, you are much more likely to use your reading skills flexibly and effectively. Also, you will probably feel happier about your studying. You will have a clear picture of what you are doing and why you are doing it. You will be in control!

Exercise

Choose from one of these:
    a book on fitness
    a book on women artists
    a book on conservation

Think and note down how you would start to read the book you have chosen if:

1 you want to get a broad idea of what it covers.
2 you want to gain detailed information about one aspect of it (eg how to get fit for a skiing holiday, or women artists of the Reformation period, or the effects of twentieth-century legislation on wildlife conservation).
3 you want to become an expert on the whole topic.
4 you want to find something on the topic which will get you interested but you don't know what that is.
5 you want to find out just one particular piece of information (eg where to buy training weights or the names of two post World War II women artists or how many giant pandas have been born in captivity).
6 you want to build up evidence which will help you to put forward a particular point of view on the topic.

Six different reasons for reading something appear in the exercise below. They give a detailed picture of what you want to gain from your reading. What you want to get out of it will indicate how you need to read.

Exercise

Draw arrows to match the purpose with the reading technique.

Purpose	*Reading technique*
finding a date (eg 1944)	reading the whole book carefully
gathering facts on one small section to support your view	using the index to start with
finding what the Corn Laws were	going quickly through the whole thing
finding a definition	reading one part carefully after using contents page/index
getting a picture of what the book is about	picking out useful parts from the index and reading them, carefully
becoming an expert on the book's content	not reading at all but running your eyes over the page looking for numbers

You may find more than one right answer.

REMEMBER
- be clear about what your purpose is
- keep it clear and in mind once you are reading

It may help if you:

Ask someone else (friend, teacher) to help you to get an idea of what you need to get from your reading.

Browse through the book you are using and see what sort of approach the author takes, what may be left out, what is definitely included, and then decide if it suits your purpose.

Try telling someone else why you are doing a piece of reading. Even if you are very unclear at the start, explaining to someone else will often help you to get your purpose clear.

Exercise

Choose a text book you have to read. Start reading and after ten minutes stop and try reading in another way (eg if you've been going slowly and carefully, try skipping through quickly). Stop again after a little while and list what you got out of reading in these two ways.

Reading gets tough when the words used are unfamiliar and the meaning doesn't seem clear. It's hard, too, when you haven't much time and feel you must get something done. If you do not have time to go through everything carefully, you may be afraid of missing something important. A lot of studying can feel like this.

So try:
- **USING THE CLUES** (see the section on magazines) to help you become more familiar with the material. This will lift your confidence.
- **SORTING OUT YOUR PURPOSE** (what you want to get out of your reading). Try to do this with the person who set the task in the first place.

REMEMBER you have a lot of reading skills available. You don't have to go through everything in the same way, or from beginning to end. Use different skills for different purposes. Experiment, both through using the exercises in this booklet and when you are studying.

NOTE MAKING

What are notes for?

People may make notes while they are reading or listening to something, or when they are thinking things up for themselves. The more you study, the more likely you are to make notes.

Why make notes? Some reasons are:

1 to help remember something which will be useful soon afterwards
2 to provide a record so that it can be used later, say in a test or examination
3 because a teacher or lecturer insists that you make notes (or because the notes will be marked!)
4 to help you concentrate on what is being read or said
5 to help get a grasp of what is being read or said, to help you to understand it
6 because everyone else seems to be doing it

Different notes for different purposes

The notes you make will probably look different depending on why you are making them.

When you make notes to help you remember soon afterwards, you will find that your memory of what you read or what was said will work quite well without lots of detail in your notes.

When you make notes to help you remember much later, you may need more detail, to help you remember accurately. If you make notes to help you revise for an examination much later, you may find that you will want to use ways of making important points stand out (eg underlining important ideas, using colour to emphasise certain parts, using arrows to point to what might be especially useful).

When you make notes to keep up your concentration, what they look like may be unimportant since you probably will not need to use them afterwards.

An important reason for making notes is to help you get a grasp of what you hear or read. When you make notes for this reason, your two major tasks are to get down what you think is important and to make some connections between ideas or pieces of information that appear to go together.

When you study, you often feel that everything in the subject is very important and you may be afraid of leaving any of it out. The fear of leaving out something crucial actually makes a lot of people write notes badly. They try to copy down whole chunks of material without making sense of it.

Make choices

Try to make some of your own choices about what is important. This is hard advice to take, but it is much better than trying to scribble down everything and failing. If you choose what sounds important to you, and look for your own links between things, at least you will have started to get a grasp of your work. You may not be totally happy with your choice but at least you have something to work with. You can, for example, use these notes to compare with someone else — to see if they agree about what is important. Or you can ask someone with a bit more authority on the subject to check if your ideas sound all right.

Part of 'John Craven's Newsround' 3/1/84

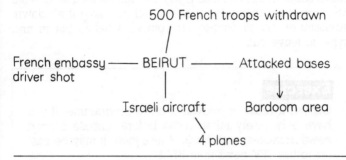

500 French troops withdrawn

French embassy —— BEIRUT —— Attacked bases
driver shot

Israeli aircraft   Bardoom area

4 planes

---

1 Bad weather in Britain

2 Chaos in Scotland - accidents on roads esp. Isle of Skye

3 Lighthouse damaged by high winds

4 S Coast wall of houses damaged by wind

5 Welsh ship driven on to rocks

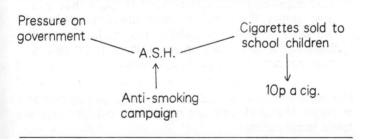

Pressure on
government   Cigarettes sold to
                             school children
          A.S.H.

                             10p a cig.
Anti-smoking
campaign

Australia ——→ hump-backed whales

                scientists have said those
                swimming off Aust. coast have
                Aust. accent!

Try the exercise below. It will force you to make notes and leave some things out. See if you can still recall a lot of what went on even though your notes will not have it all down. Remember, try to choose for yourself what to put in and what to leave out.

Exercise

Choose a radio or television news programme. If you have only rarely taken notes before, choose a short news broadcast from Radio 4 as a start. It may be easier to use ITV news than BBC.

Make notes during the programme. Warning! The news can be read quite quickly, so you are going to have to choose what to note. Put down what *you* feel is important. Make your own choices. Don't try to get it all.

When the programme is over, take a look at your notes. How did you do? Can you remember most of what happened? Do you remember more than you have written? If you can, you have already proved you can use your notes intelligently. You will find you use them almost like hooks on which to hang the rest of what you have heard or thought about.

Examples of notes are included on the page opposite and on pages 41 and 44. They are not perfect, but they show we made some choices.

Exercise

Compare your notes with ours. List what you like about both sets of notes.

If you can borrow notes from friends, it is useful to compare their notes with yours too.

9 'O' Clock

ISRAEL JETS STRIKE
100+ killed in Lebanon, Bekka Valley – revenge attack on
Muslim group there. 16 jets involved for an hour. Mostly
civilian casualties. Syrian helicopters help to evacuate.
Threats of reprisals.
   Lt R Goodman (released POW) gets back to USA with
Rev. Jackson

ALL-OUT SHIPYARDS STRIKE NOW LIKELY
ACAS talks break down. Management will discuss
productivity but keep to tough line, hoping for a patchy strike.

£ FALLS AGAIN ON FOREIGN EXCHANGES
1 cent down against $. Steady against other currencies.

LORD CHANCELLOR APOLOGISES TO WOOLWORTHS
Woolworths had been criticised for prosecuting pensioner.
The 'Recorder' had said W/Ws were wrong. Hailsham
called the comments 'intemperate'.

DOCTORS' DEPUTIES : BMA RESPONDS
Agencies have been under fire: doctors inexperienced and
worked too hard. Govt. proposed to clamp down a month
ago. BMA wants guidelines changed.

FIGHTS AT TALBOT FACTORY IN FRANCE
Unions disagree over accepting management redundancy
plans

TUNISIA (FOOD) RIOTS CONTINUE
Curfew operates. Things getting calmer. British
holiday committee urges tourist caution.

NIGERIA
New rulers criticise old economic policies.

DRUG SMUGGLING
More seizures than ever last year: less cannabis, more
cocaine

MOTORIST SHOT LAST NIGHT
by a gunman is now stable. Shotgun wound

MRS JANICE WESTON left £400,000+ – murdered
last year

POLICE ANNOUNCE BETTER FORCE LINKS new rules in
operation

SCOTTISH HOMES STILL LACK IN ELECTRICITY 2 days
after storms

DENNIS LILLEE retires

Liverpool sextuplets   A ⎫
Winter takes over - storms   B ⎬ headlines
Freed by Syrians - US Airman   C ⎪
Yorks boy reunited with father   ⎭

A   (1)   SEXTUPLETS ——— 1st view on TV

            Walton babies

                                    worst weather
                                    power lines down
                                         ↓
B   (2)   WINTER STORMS eg Scots highland
                                         Welsh coast
Hazardous rds esp
Shapfell area   rescue of crew of 6 from
     ↓   tanker nr Milford Haven
Speed restrictions   ↓
+ lanes closed
                                 Cresswell on Northumb coast:
                                 winds of 92 mph

C   (3)   Lt R Goodman US airman
                    ↓
            set free in Lebanon
                    ↓
            ∴ Jesse Jackson's campaign
                    ↑
JJ accused of trying to get votes in
this way but he denies this

44

Exercise

Choose one or two pages of a text book or novel you are studying. Make notes on what is in these pages. Use coloured pens or felt tips to draw boxes around or underline headings and important words in your notes.

Does this make them easier to read?
Does this help you to remember what's in them?

Exercise

Re-write your notes using a different technique.

Use a star pattern (see page 18) if you didn't use it first time;

or

write your notes as brief jottings under headings;

or

write one paragraph of notes without using any headings except the title, and covering each line completely, like the lines of writing in a book.

Decide which technique you prefer, and jot down when you would use it and when you wouldn't.
The technique I prefer is ....
I would use it when ....
I would not use it for ....

Notes

HELP YOURSELF TO WRITE BETTER

Writing in different ways for different purposes

As a student, you may often use writing as a way of expressing your thoughts and feelings. Our writing reflects our thinking. If you are having trouble writing, it may be that you haven't got your thoughts together.

Before you can write clearly, your thinking must be clear

Again, your purposes for writing are important. You can use writing as a way of getting your thoughts clearer. That's fine and can be very productive. But if you are using writing to tell someone something, for example in an essay or examination answer, then you will probably need to have many of your thoughts clear **before** you write the actual answer.

Writing can help YOU
- **to get your thoughts clear**
- **to explore some of your ideas**
- **to remind yourself of important points**

or it may be for SOMEONE ELSE
- **a teacher**
- **an examiner**
- **a supervisor**

Exercise

Have a look at the following statements:

> got up at 8.30
> the bathroom
> the door knob turned

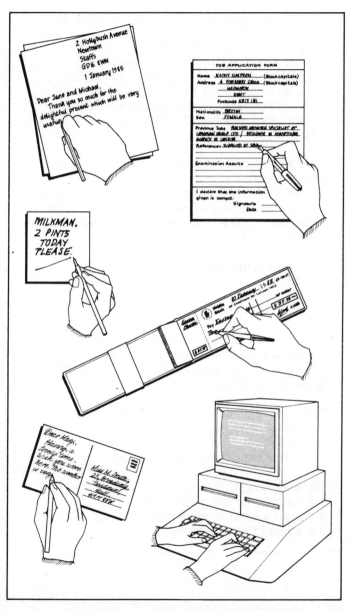

Writing

We imagined that we were writing a thriller and put these together like this:

I got up at 8.30, bleary-eyed and ill-tempered as usual. I had just reached the landing when I first heard the noise — a faint scratching sort of sound and it was coming from the direction of the bathroom. My skin prickled and I moved slowly down the corridor. As I reached the bathroom the door knob turned . . .

Then we put ourselves into the shoes of a policeman giving evidence in court:

Miss X rose at 8.30 a.m. She left her bedroom and, at a brisk pace, proceeded towards the bathroom. As she approached, she reported that the door knob turned.

Then we put the statements in note form:
1 Up 8.30
2 To bthrm
3 B.drknob turned.

These are all simple examples of the ways in which we can use the same basic materials in different ways according to our purposes. *When you write, you have to decide on your own purposes.*

Try to link the following statements:
it was a hot air balloon
they fell out
the occupants were unusual

Write as though you are:
1 a reporter for the local påper
2 writing a letter to someone in hospital
3 a writer of mystery stories

Writing as part of studying

When you are writing an essay, a project or an exam answer, you are usually expected to write in a certain way. It helps to learn as much as you can about what is expected.

You have to learn, for example, what the person who marks or assesses your work wants. What does he or she give marks for? How long should your work be? Can you find any examples of what the work should sound like? Should there be any comments like 'I think' in what you produce? Are notes acceptable at times? Do you need to show you have researched other things? Do you have to sound like an historian, a scientist, or someone else? How much factual information must you put in?

You can find the answer to such questions as these:
- by asking
- **by looking at clues available in work you have already finished and had marked**
- **by comparing your work with that of others to see what does well and what badly**

If you can, ask whoever assesses or marks your work. They may not be able to give you a simple answer and they may say it has a lot to do with the way you arrange what you have to say. This brings us on to a second point about writing.

One of the more difficult things to do when you are writing as part of your studying is to make your work 'hang together'.

Choosing an order for your ideas when you write

There usually has to be some order in the way you put your thoughts together when you write as a student. Your writing should usually follow some pattern, although you can vary that pattern quite a lot.

When writing essays and examination answers:
- you have a selection of information or ideas (perhaps they are facts, possibly thoughts)
- you have the subject or topic that holds the information together
- you have ways of making statements or creating an impression by changing slightly the words you use and the ways you use them

Keep one eye on the order you have chosen and the other on how you fasten things together. There are always different ways in which your ideas can be arranged, but once you've chosen an order, keep to it. Choose the order according to your purpose and your knowledge of what your reader expects.

Make sure your order:
1 fits in with your purpose, so that you are fairly clear what you want to do
2 fits in with what you've been asked to do
3 makes sense to your reader
4 fits around all of what you want to include (so that you aren't tempted to swap to another way of writing half way through)

Exercise

Write three paragraphs about yourself (or take another topic that you can write about fairly easily, perhaps where you live, or someone you know, or something you enjoy doing) including a few different items or past events that you feel have been important.

The first time you write, try to use a time sequence to decide what you'll put in the first, second and third paragraphs. Either put the most recent thing last and work backwards towards it, or put the most recent thing first.

Then, using the same items or events, decide on a different arrangement and write. You could try putting what you feel is the most important thing first, and then continuing. Or you could start with something that made you happy or amused and then contrast it with something sadder.

This exercise will show you that as well as being able to use different styles (as you did with the hot air balloon) you can use quite different arrangements.

Writing

USING YOUR SKILLS

1 for homework
2 for essays
3 for projects
4 for exam revision

Homework — getting started

When you've got homework to do, you have to think about:
- what you're going to do
- when you're going to do it

Your time is valuable. You may have a deadline to work to. In the end you're going to have to get down to it. Try these ideas to help you get started. Decide how much there is to do.

If there is a lot to do

Try to break it into parts, eg French, Physics, Maths, or Chapters 1 and 2.

Make a guess at how long each part will take.

Make out a plan giving the time when you'll be doing each bit of the work. (Don't be too ambitious — you've probably got other things you need or want to do!)

Even if you can't make a plan, begin on something. Stop after 20 minutes and see if you can do a plan once you've got going.

Tick off the sections or subjects you've finished, so that you can see you are making progress.

If there is a bit to do

Don't keep putting it off, because there's not all that much to do.

Make a deal with yourself — fix a time when you'll start work, and write that down where you (and perhaps someone else) can see it.

Decide roughly what time you'll stop, so that you know when you will be free to do something else.

If you can't get started . . .

Try talking about it to someone else or if there's no one to talk to, try jotting down *why* you can't get started — sometimes doing that will be enough to make you feel you can start. (But be careful not to do these things just to put work off longer!)

When you've got to do homework, you'll need to:
- **Think about what you have to do — make sure you are clear about the question or topic or exercise. (Try writing it out again in your own words.)**
- **Decide if you need anything such as more information before you get started.**
- **Decide on a time schedule.**

Using your skills

Think about the homework you've been set soon after you've been given it. Ask questions in class or talk it over with a friend as soon as possible. Being clear about the task helps enormously.

This is the star pattern with some detail included. Perhaps we've left out things which seem important to you.

Star pattern on homework

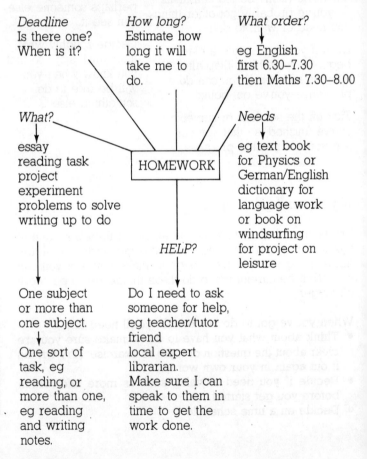

Deadline
Is there one?
When is it?

How long?
Estimate how
long it will
take me to
do.

What order?
↓
eg English
first 6.30–7.30
then Maths 7.30–8.00

What?
↓
essay
reading task
project
experiment
problems to solve
writing up to do

HOMEWORK

Needs
↓
eg text book
for Physics or
German/English
dictionary for
language work
or book on
windsurfing
for project on
leisure

HELP?

One subject
or more than
one subject.
↓
One sort of
task, eg
reading, or
more than one,
eg reading
and writing
notes.

Do I need to ask
someone for help,
eg teacher/tutor
friend
local expert
librarian.
Make sure I can
speak to them in
time to get the
work done.

Essays — questions to help you

Homework may involve writing essays, or you may be writing essays at college or at school or in an exam.

When you have an essay to do, think about:
- **WHAT you are being asked to do**
- **HOW you are going to do it**

Here's a list of questions you may find it useful to ask yourself and to jot down answers for, when you've got an essay to write.

1 *What is the question?* eg does it mean write whatever I know about the topic, or is it asking me to support a theory, or what?

2 *Who is going to read it?* What audience am I writing for? Can I guess at what the marker is looking for and what they expect in terms of style and content?

3 *In what order will I say what I've got to say?* Does the question decide this for me or have I got to decide what seems logical? What goes with what?

4 *Do I find it useful to start with a plan?* Have I found this worked for me in the past? Are my ideas clear enough to start a plan?

5 *Do I find it useful to do some writing before I start planning what goes where?* Does actually writing something down help me to get my thoughts clear? Can I then decide how the whole thing should be put together?

6 *How much have I got to write?* Is there a specified length?

Using your skills

Some things to check on while you're writing and when you've got to the end are:

- Does it say what I mean?
- Does it do what it needs to?
- Is it clear?
- Is there a sequence? (that is sensible, logical order)
- Is there enough?
- Is there too much?
- Have I been careful to use complete sentences all through?
- Have I started a new paragraph where I needed to? (that is with a fresh set of ideas or a new slant on the topic)

Like all studying, there is not just one right or one wrong way to write an essay. Find a way that works for you. This means two things:

- that you feel happy with your method
- that it gets you the sort of marks you want and expect.

Although there is no one way of doing essays, the end product does have to conform to certain standards which are set by other people. When you get an essay back once it's been marked, read all the comments carefully. These comments provide valuable clues to what is required.

Projects — deciding what to do and how to do it

The size of a project can be frightening. In a project you probably have to use skills in all the areas we have mentioned in this book.

Suggestions to help you begin

Do you have a choice about the topic, or not?
If you have a choice, think carefully about what you are going to do. Try to balance your own interests with those of your likely audience. Take into account how easy it is going to be to find information on the topic you choose. Don't be too quick to pick what will be very easy; you might get bored, and so might whoever reads it.

If you do not have a choice and have been told to do something in particular, spend some time thinking about the topic. What does it mean? What does the person who will mark it expect you to cover? How could you break the thing up into different parts? How might the parts link together?

Do you have to make a firm plan?
Someone may ask you to make a very detailed plan, but this is not always the best way to start. Once you have your topic, try browsing through a few information sources (books, library, an electronic source). Get an idea of the types of things that go together in this topic. Only when you have some idea about the topic in general can you start to ask good questions and plan what to include.

A star pattern (see page 18) may help you to decide on areas to work at in the project. It may also help you to see some links between different parts of the project. Don't be afraid to make your own choices about how the project is going to be chopped up. And if it suddenly seems that the project is going to be colossal if you include everything, make up your mind that you will only include what you feel is important. Make choices and if you feel unsure about them, go and talk about them with someone else.

How do I get started?

It is probably not very important where you begin. It is only important that you make a start quite early and give yourself some time to complete a reasonable amount. You certainly don't have to start with an introduction, because you are unlikely to know exactly what you are introducing! Remember that once you start, you don't have to treat everything you do as a finished product to fit into a precise place in the project. You should be prepared to re-write things if you want. You should expect to re-plan bits of the project from time to time. Keep in mind why you are doing it and what your audience is going to expect.

What do I do?

You will do all the things we have mentioned in this booklet:
**THINK ABOUT INFORMATION (and ASK QUESTIONS),
FIND INFORMATION, READ IT, probably MAKE NOTES
and WRITE.** *Remember*, **you don't have to do these in this
order.** You can go backwards and forwards, adding or
improving things as you wish.

How do I put it together?

You will want to produce something which shows what you
think about the topic. You will have your own order. Make
your own decisions but keep an eye on what the reader will
think, too. Remember that you do not always have to write
a project — you may be allowed to present it in another way,
perhaps as photographs and a tape. Find out what is
allowed.

Exams — what to do before the exam: being prepared

There are things you can do before the exam date, and
things which are relevant to actually doing the exam.

Before the exam

Find out:
- How long will it be?
- What sort? (eg essay, multiple choice, problems to solve)
- Where will it be?
- Is there a past paper or papers to look at?
- What might come up?
- Will my main task be to:
  memorise
  or understand
  or a combination of these?

Before the exam

Collect all you have
- your notes
- your essays
- your answers
- your text books
- and especially *YOU* — you have been working on the subject and may well know more about it than you have written down

Use all of these to get a good overall picture.

You may want to *condense* your notes and take brief notes from your other work.

You will need to revise. Writing down the times you can revise and what you need to do at these times can help enormously.

REMEMBER Feelings always come into learning, both good feelings and bad ones depending on you and lots of other factors like the relevance of the subject to you and how well or badly it's taught. Exam times can spark off bad feelings. We all share worries about the possibility of not doing as well as we could. Worry and fear can tighten us up, and stop us using skills we've got. We may just write down anything we can think of, or find our minds a blank, or stop reading the questions carefully and lose sight of our purpose. All these things can happen and do happen to people. BUT there are ways of helping to see they don't happen to you.

Using your skills

Before the exam

1 Practise doing 'mock' exams under exam conditions.
2 Picture yourself in the exam and develop a clear picture of yourself being calm and being able to use your skills and knowledge. Try and do this picturing exercise each day for at least the week before the exam.
3 Test yourself on things likely to come up, or better still find someone else to test you.
4 Practise doing written work in the time you'll have in the exam.
5 Talk about your queries — 'What do you do if . . .' — in class and/or with friends.

REMEMBER Probably everyone doing an exam is a bit nervous, and, believe it or not, a bit of anxiety can actually help you to do well!

INDEX

Index